GW00726035

Inspired

by

Outlaws

Les Merton

Published by Palores Publications 2006

Les Merton
Inspired by Outlaws

ISBN   0-9551878-4-2
ISBN   978-0-9551878-4-1

Published by:

Palores Publications,
11a Penryn Street,
Redruth,
Cornwall.
TR15 2SP

Designed and printed by:

Imageset,
63 Tehidy Road,
Camborne,
Cornwall.
TR14 8LJ

Typeset in:

Times 11pt
Tahoma 18pt

Inspired

by

Outlaws

Les Merton

if you believe you're a poet, then you're saved
Gregory Corso

Inspired by Outlaws

Inspired by Outlaws

Author's Note

This collection title, Inspired by Outlaws, deserves explaining. The embryo idea for this collection came from reading the excellent poetry magazine, Outlaw, edited by Bryn Fortey, which I found to be very inspirational.

Thanks to

Bev Hewett, Mike Chapple, for their part in this production. Mick Paynter for being there to provide feedback and to Joe Speer, Bryn Fortey, Andrew Nightingale, Tony Lamb, Jane Tozer and Loveday Jenkin.

Acknowledgements

It is the custom with poetry collections to list and acknowledge magazines, anthologies and internet sites where the poems, published in the collection, have appeared previously. Unfortunately I do not have a full list of where some of the previously publish poems have appeared. This is due to my home and all poetry records being destroyed by fire in March 2005. Rather than name some and miss others, I would just like to acknowledge all the magazines anthologies and internet sites that have been kind enough to publish my writing over the years.

Dedication

this collection
is dedicated to
outlaws of the mind

Definitions
(leading to beat reality)

beat -
a main accent in music or poetry

reality -
a fact

beat -
a member of the beat generation; a nonconformist in dress and behaviour

reality -
real existence; the state of being real

beat -
The adjective "beat" (introduced by Herbert Huncke) had the connotations of "tired" or "down and out", but Jack Kerouac added the paradoxical connotations of "upbeat", "beatific"*, and the musical association of being "on the beat"

*In Roman Catholic theology, the beatific vision is the direct perception of God enjoyed by those who are in Heaven, imparting supreme happiness or blessedness

reality -
the state of things as they are, rather than as they are imagined to be

beats - a United States youth subculture of the 1950s; rejected possessions or regular work or traditional dress for communal living and psychedelic drugs and anarchism; favoured modern forms of jazz (e.g. bebop)

reality -
in its most liberal sense, includes everything that is, whether or not it is observable, accessible or understandable by science, philosophy, theology or any other system of analysis. Reality in this sense may include both being and nothingness

the beat generation -
young people who did not follow accepted principles and customs but who valued personal experience instead

eat reality -
erm any combination of beat and reality

eat reality -
hat is or what has been or what might be, perceptive usually outside of
onvention, realistically converted to poetic truth, full of intense conviction
nd raw consciousness

eat reality -
elf discovery rejected by society

eat reality -
 social comment on life

Contents

Contents

Inspired by Outlaws

ool hand

rolled sex
cross black and white keys

is fingers
new highs and lows

f down and out days
hen sound

as all there was
etween lust and loneliness

biography of a generation

an itch
that became a life force

hallucinating
the very heart

of hip, beat,
cool and rock on

writers and poets
who led a movement

pounded a piano
or bowed the bass

they were riders of rails
buffs of the open road

bar room cowboys
forging outlaw trails

they hugged reality
ignored ticking clocks

ved and made love
street corner angels

ave time
orphans and strays

ft memories
camp fire flames

ey knew God's hour
as a special time

nd discovered their destiny
ne early dawn

when they took a journey
ut of the abyss

voided
he four horsemen

o become
heir own ferrymen

Scarface

*There is one certainty in the future of a people
of the resources, intelligence, and character
of the people of the United States - that is prosperity.*
                    Herbert Hoover; May 1930

They called him a bootlegger.
Al Capone don't deny it.

He admitted it's bootleg
while it's on the trucks.

But, when you're a host at the club
or any other joint it's hospitality.

Maybe one type of logic,
ran foul of another

that came with a name borrowed
from India the Untouchables.

And then it was legal

I think this would be a good time for beer.
Franklin D. Roosevelt; March 12, 1933

A legal foamy flood
with giant waves of celebration
swept through the so called dry land.

Newspapers were swamped with the story:
Prohibition was over - alcohol was legitimate,
and here to stay they said.

Those behind the scenes
were gushing as they speculated
on the income from extra taxes.

And then there were the psychologists
who studied the effects of the people
who thought they were having a good time...

Downtown

In early hours,
day and night hide behind
neon signs and urban gloss.

Air is intense with filtering
madness; reality wallows
in banks of pollution.

Streets are thinner, tighter:
pack animals guard territory
with predatory instinct.

In a regenerated building,
masked with heavy shades,
a ray of light slices shadow...

Road Movie

A car is a car - a stolen car is something else -
a fantasy in its own right: freedom, with wheels
to burn and an illuminated speedo that will hit
a ton fifty in a smooth foot to floor movement.

A girl is a girl - a hitch hiking girl is something else -
a fantasy in her own right: thumbing opportunity
with an I-want-a-ride smile, that will tempt
driving into the sunset into looking for lay-bys.

A road is a road - an infinite road is something else -
a fantasy in its own right: going into the unknown
beyond dreams, previous experience, stimulating
a reason for living in days without end.

A movie is a movie - a road movie is something else -
a fantasy in its own right: black and white images
storytelling flickers, highs and lows, plot planned
to climax in ninety seven minutes with, I told you so.

A crash is a crash - a deliberate crash is something else -
a fantasy in its own right: togetherness for ever.
Two dead bodies in a burnt out stolen car
and a newspaper epitaph, Inexplicable Accident.

And The Children

And the children:
guzzle beer,
swig bottles of wine,
swallow spirits neat.

And the children:
smoke,
enjoy ecstasy,
snort white lines.

And the children:
isolated,
misunderstood,
gather in gangs.

And the children:
bond
by fornicating
in the streets.

And the children:
respect
the wild and corrupt
who lead them.

And the children:
machine gun
obscenity,
and distill hatred.

And the children:
pick pocket,
shop lift, ram-raid,
mug, and terroriswe.

And the children:
gather
guns, knives, clubs,
they are ready.

And the children:
are anonymous
martyrs buried
in mass graves.

And the children:
are cult worshipped
by the next generation;
and these children...

The Bar

some place downtown
where streets slide into gloom.

The bar with its neon name
like nick, slick or candle wick.

The bar with depth and feeling,
good booze and good company.

The bar where she sat
on a high stool, real cool, no fool.

The bar where her legs tempt
more than a bitch on heat.

The bar where at thirteen
she was old, cold and sold.

The bar some place downtown
where they play blues all night.

In Vain
(after Jack Kerouac)

Walking a Holy Cow
      through Macdonalds
           in vain

Showering the White House
      with messages of peace
           in vain

Reading the Bible
      looking for truth
           in vain

Falling in love
      expecting...
           in vain

Writing, rewriting, editing,
      proofing, editing, rewriting
           in vain

All the Gods, all the prophets
      all the beliefs, all the faiths
           in vain

Buddy, can you spare a dime?

*We have been passing through
one of those great economic storms
which periodically bring hardship
and suffering upon our people.*
                        Herbert Hoover; May, 1930

I don't know how many times I asked,
'Buddy, can you spare a dime?'

I don't remember how many times
I was turned down.

I do remember one time
when some guy in a suit

that had seen better days
stared at me for a while and nodded.

I mumbled thanks, avoided
his eyes and moved away.

She must have been watching
from where she was sitting on the stoop

as I walked by,
she lifted her skirt and said,

          'How about it?'

I replied honestly,
'Sorry babe, I'd rather eat.'

Voody

rote, played and sung his way
rough social history of his time:
arted an anthem, created a legend.

is land, through your life,
ke a whiff, talkin' blues
esus Christ! It was hard travelling...

Voody observing, being personal -
olitics would find their way
nd if you ain't got no home

ravelling is the way
p down and across the USA
eeing disaster and everyday lives

f folk who didn't have the do re mi.
Going down that road, working hard...
eeling bad... so long...

t's been good to know you...
eep your skillet good and greasy,
on't hit the skids on the old skid row

Voody...

Smokey's Café Cameos

A well fed jukebox belches
anarchy into an oppressed atmosphere.

In a dark alcove, two acne teens grope
each other with primeval instincts.

A hippy group of Dylan students
burn and rave, into that good night.

Ghosts of customers past watch
from a mirror advertising drinking chocolate.

Sapped by fading magic a street angel
worries about the lack of new tricks.

A Cockney lorry driver tries ordering
a rosy and peckham from a Greek waitress.

A labyrinth of cracks in the walls,
are graffiti titled, *after Jackson Pollock.*

The marooned hitch-hiker sits
willing wheels to come his way.

A canvasser swigs courage, to face the animal
public, from a bottle in a brown paper bag.

The pendulum swings a greasy arc,
all day breakfasts are served around the clock.

Monday Evening - Redruth

From an embankment fir tree,
the magpie's call sounds like machine gun fire.

An army of dark clouds position
behind Carn Brea, and the drummer in a band
that will never make it beyond practice sessions,
rolls thunder across roof tops.

A boy racer burns rubber
squealing to stop at red lights,
revving the highly tuned engine louder
than the thump-thump of his sound system heart.

On orange he accelerates,
from naught to his sunset in sixty seconds.

it suited me

smoke was thick
sweat was cool
old wail on
just did his thing

and you wriggled
ass - tight ass baby -
in jeans that shrunk
beneath your skin

moving sex
dancing freedom -
it suited me
to watch...

and listen...
as old wail on
blew up more
in encore after encore

News any which way but easy

How happy to be a citizen,
Where the voice of the people rules.
                    The Happy American; song; Anonymous, 1926

Standing
under street light warmth,
reading discarded newspapers:

> *Eleanor Roosevelt*
> *does voluntary work*
> *in soup kitchens.*

Hitching
to see poverty
in a different location.
The truck driver said:

> *IOUs are appearing*
> *on collection plates*
> *in churches.*

Riding
the rails listening
to box car blues:

> *John D Rockefeller*
> *giving out dimes*
> *all with the same message*
> *from Lincoln:*
> *'In God We Trust Liberty.'*

News
any which way but easy...

Railway Station Morning

the rustle
of yesterday's news
keeps a little warmth in
keeps a lot of cold out

the sound
of approaching steam
gives a bite of the faith
gives a rhyme for season

the song
of the hobo
is folk-blues tales
is riding the rails - the rails

Day out in Bartow

All around you are signs
repeating the magic phrase:
Drink Coca-Cola
          Erskine Caldwell; January, 1934

It's another day out
for families from Bartow, Georgia.

No one has any spare cash
but days like this make life more bearable.

Someone will know the words
and start singing the Woody Guthrie song:

        End o' my line, end o' my line...

We all knew Woody was singing
about dust storms

but the song seems appropriate:
sets the tone for the afternoon's show.

Some nigger, we heard,
didn't show proper respect for white folks;

he was sorted.
Now, it's time to string him up.

Only trouble is
all day long our kids will be asking

for a Coke. There ought to be a law:
banning 'Coca-Cola' advertising.

Kings Cross Railway Station

Dossing is possible at Kings Cross.
Sheets from the Financial Times
between clothing layers hold body heat.
They say the pink newspaper keeps
you warmer than any other daily.

Dossers can be moved on...
however, the cops never arrest
anyone: nights in nick are like being
at The Hilton when your strapped.

Rossers can be cool:
they give out odd fags
and have a quiet drag, before telling
you to be gone by six in the morning.

With a bit of foresight and luck,
enough bread has been kept back
for a roadside rosy and peckham...

Then it's on to the big stores,
libraries, churches, bus stations,
galleries, anywhere warm - before
being on the lunch hour pitch:

Got any spare coins for a cup of tea.

... If everyone was to give just a bit
of loose change, you'd live like a king...

Shebeen

ock steady to reggae, moonshine,
oints, stacked cards, an argument -

rick shithouses stopped
he fight and helped me exit:

 bounced down the stairs
vithout breaking a bone;

ead butted the fire door and whirled
ike a dervish into waiting arms...

e appreciated my efforts and returned
he gesture by charging me with

vilfully obstructing a police officer
n the execution of his duties.

Wandering Camborne Streets

*(this poem was written when I was homeless
and living in a hostel in Camborne - unfortunately
the sentiments expressed applies to many towns)*

WH Smith, Costcutter,
Oxfam, Barclays, Co-op...

Specsavers, Clic, Argos,
Woolworth, Wimpy, Boots...

Superdrug, Dorothy Perkins,
Halifax, Nationwide, Tesco...

a clone
of everywhere and anywhere

*apart from what one sees walking
streets paved with Chinese granite*

*there is what one hears:
the incestuous offspring*

*of soap opera accents
mutating local dialects.*

Survivor

Mamma don't know bout his music
or how he broke jail before his trial
never realised her poor boy's hunger
all she saw was his strutting style.

He took off in the dark of midnight
to escape the sheriff's overdues
hitch the highway to the border
and bided time singing the blues.

He worked his passage down river
melancholy waved him good bye
with the sad words of his song
and the drowned tear in his eye.

The solitude of the box car
over sleepers and well worn rails
with no-one to talk to, thoughts
were freedom in mouth organ tales.

He spent a while in Memphis,
did a gig for cross-dressed queens
odd jobbed in San Francisco
fore he settled in New Orleans.

He rode out that ole hurricane
as others got swept away by tide
he had nothing left to stay put for
so destiny became his travel guide.

Before a Naked Lunch

I am forced to the appalling conclusion
that I would have never become a writer but for Joan's death
William S Burroughs 1953

soft and feminine Joan Vollmer -
      escaped from the shackles of the late 1930s American household
            and its social mores to find sexual and intellectual freedom -

common law wife -
      resentful and contemptuous of Burroughs's -
            unconventional and adventurous young lady -

Benzedrines for kicks
      Joan became tragically attracted to the uppers,
            and degenerated into a state of addiction -

Mexico City -
      Joan could no longer get Benzedrine,
            and made do with cheap tequila

Burroughs loved guns
      he had an ever increasing lack of intimacy
            and reliance on heroin -

Joan had the uncanny ability to receive images
      that Bill sent her telepathically...
            - a party - William Tell -

.38-caliber automatic pistol
      "I can't look," Joan said.
            "You know I can't stand the sight of blood."

Cut and Paste Before a Naked Lunch

The road of excess leads to the palace of wisdom.
William Blake

The act of writing is complex - a montage of fragments -

tequila -
.38-caliber automatic pistol -
a drinking glass -

one shot -
an unbroken glass rolling on the floor -
a body -
soft and feminine -

Murder Charges...

Mexico City:-
on the evening of September 6, 1951,
a 37-year-old American man fatally shot
his ten-years-younger American wife in the forehead
with a .38-caliber automatic pistol,
while aiming at a drinking glass
balanced on top of her head.

tequila - .38-caliber automatic pistol - soft and feminine - a drinking glass -
one shot *not as straight as an arrow* - an unbroken glass rolling on the floor -
a body - murder charges...
impetus for a literary career...

The act of writing is complex - a montage of fragments -

Joan Vollmer Adams Burroughs
was not an artist or writer,
but
William S Burroughs
and others credit her
with being a powerful inspiration
to their work.

Business

He flashed gold,
puffed a Havana cigar:
believed that his latest
put him in executive class.

The girl, a tousled blonde
with a nymph-like-body,
sat on a bar stool revealing
tense slender legs... .

She chain smoked,
pouted between drags,
and gave every man in the bar
a look with come-to-bed eyes.

Her posture was less inviting:
too many persuasive kicks
from the new pimp made
suggestive movements painful.

Cockney Steve

was clean:
he hung out with us for a while.

Briefly mentioned
his days as a butcher.

Our scene wasn't really him.
Most times he just listened.

On the subject of smoking,
he had a classic...

'My mate never smoked!
And he died of cancer... .

He used to chew that gum...

Come to find out
it was nicotine gum.'

Depression?

*These really are good times
but only a few know it.*
                    Henry Ford; March, 1930

There is no work,
I have to survive...

I learn to wait in breadlines
and queue for soup kitchens

I tramp the sidewalks,
for daily hand to mouth living;

my feet are swollen and blistered
with going from one charity to another

there is no work...
I walk to eat - eat to walk.

I sleep in doorways,
on park benches. And when I can

on the corner seat of a train
running continuously between

Times Square and Coney Island.
Occasionally there's the luxury

of Grand Central Terminal
where I wash for a nickel...

'God Bless America.'

Local Nick

Inside the cell it's stark.
Four walls - a locked door
a barred window and a high ceiling.

And, some mother's left a message
on the ceiling - *Don't let it get to U.*
Beats me how they get up there.

Crapping is real crap in here:
they watch you through the peep hole
and love catching you with your pants down...

Bastards! It doesn't matter how
many times you ring they won't answer
to push the flush button outside the cell.

There is also stench from the mattress
not quite strong enough to knock you out -
still got to rely on a hand job.

Hand jobs are suicide of the mind.

Fancy

       had a pitch between
New Street Station and the Market.
He also cruised a few hot spots.

Fancy always greeted with,
'Do you fancy something fancy,'

and gave his hormone breasts
a jiggle - a smile would return
'a bit of what you fancy...'

before he spun smoothly
on his high heels so you could
eye him up from behind.

Many a red blooded man
was deceived by Fancy's
mini skirted back view.

These days not even
those who swing both ways
fancy, Fancy... .

He's got, pay the price,
a positive tag - he and the she
in him are just wasting away.

Fat Man

Fat Man's walked in from the country,
in his down at heel, toe peeping shoes
carrying his pride with nothing to lose.

Fat Man's walked in from the country,
trouser turn-ups full of grass seed
but he's a Man's man with any creed.

Fat Man's walked in from the country,
shirt sleeves rolled-up past the elbow
even though he's abandoned the plough.

Fat Man's walked in from the country,
don't cost nothing to shoot the breeze
or to sit and tease black-n-white keys.

Fat Man's walked in from the country,
reckon everything that he's got he has,
now he's playing New Orleans' jazz.

Dick The Gypsy

created by hard times -
down and out in Mosside
without even a ha' penny
to scratch his ass.

Rows of terraced houses
most of them occupied
with daughters, mothers,
grannies who wanted

to believe,
there was something better
just around the corner,
tomorrow, next week,

next month, next year.
Something better,
sometime, somewhere:

Tell your fortune lady,
Just cross my palm with silver.

St Ives Festival

September Friday
that would have done
justice to the season.

The heart of Downalong,
pumps life blood through
festival arteries:

Blues music, folk guitar
song, a poem, a tale...
live from Norway Square.

Regular voices,
up country accents,
Manchester, London,
Birmingham you name it.

The St Ives in crowd
attract their own kind;
who love it - it's arty,
the Cornish are great... .

And there's galleries
to impulse buy paintings
of fishing boats to match
home lounge colour schemes.

Gulls dive and thrive
on pasties and ice cream,
and a man hovers: he'll do
his own down if needs must.

The Power of Trains

that click over the rails,
the hoot of the whistle,
the sight,
the smell,
stream.

whether you're coming home
or going away,
there's that thing
about trains.

something else too;
when you live near
to a railway line,
the sound of coming
and going of trains
is a comfort,

if you move away
from that sound;
sleepless nights,
and moody days follow
there's no explaining it
that's the power of trains.

Dust

Now I lay me down to snore,
tons of dust in every pore.
The Dust Bowl Song; Anonymous; 1935

Time to move on.

When you blink, bite,
breath, eat, sleep, shit
and think dust... .

Time to move on.

Heat, drought, insects,
and more dust, it feels like
the apocalypse... .

Time to move on.

The horizon is lost behind
clouds of dust, somewhere
a blue sun tries to shine... .

Time to move on.

No birds, no animals,
empty shacks everywhere.
No life for miles... .

Ronald

In the last school year photograph,
Ronald's face was slightly in profile.
He couldn't get away with anymore
under supervisions of a, 'stand straight,
look front, be proud of your school, or
I'll scat you on your ass,' headmaster.

Convinced he knew his best side,
positive he would be a somebody.
Ronald left school in flamboyant style:
he bought a pair of leather gloves,
one to wear and one to flick.

In a city, miles from country roots,
Ronald discovered his artistic gift;
he could sketch teenage idols
film stars and equally popular
public figures from memory.

He traded from any vacant stretch
of pavement, between Woolworth's
and the Co-op, that wasn't under
the eye of the bobby on the beat.

Image came from laziness. Ronald
stopped shaving, grew his hair long,
He walked everywhere: all the buses
refused entry to the hairy individual
who wore a frock coat with a skull,
of a dead bird, hanging from his lapel.

Confident his ability equalled the talent
of Vincent van Gogh and not fancying
cutting off a ear to emulate the artist.
Ronald decided to create his version
of Crows Over A Cornfield.

ter appropriating a sheaf of corn,
ɔnald attached it by mud washed
a large canvass. His plan was simple,
would go out, shoot a few crows
ing them home and suspend them
ove the corn...

ɔnald was found in a field, dead.
ɛ had been shot in the head.
ɪe gun lay at his side.

edia headlines sensationalised... .
ɔcentric artist found dead! Murder?
ɪicide? Or death by misadventure?

he hunt was on for a photograph
ʾ Ronald. The one taken in the field
ith his face artistically rearranged
ɣ the shotgun blast was rejected.

he only photograph to be found
as the school one with his face
ι profile. It was ideal, especially
ɔr a story with an enigma...

ɪd an unwritten epitaph: poser.

protest

through hunger
into pain and out again

know
you are not fasting

realise
starvation begins

when the body
has fed off itself

clarity is vision
vision is clarity

moving
nearer and nearer

to the sound
of the piper

with one last act
of defiance

atisfaction

a fogged out
le street who cares.

ere down - way down
e social scale,

s blues and cruising,
oking for skin tight sex.

ot to get some... .
atisfaction.

atisfaction... like blowing
smoke ring from a sawn off.

Paint It Grey

rain drips
through missing slates
plip plop sounds in a tin bowl
will never make gospel or soul

paint it grey
it ain't going to go away

when crops don't survive
belts tighten another notch
sweet smells from across the street
will never be ours to eat

paint it grey
dirt farming doesn't pay

music men only know
songs of life, bitter sweet,
full of strife, blue as blue
shanty town through and through

paint it grey
the future's worse than yesterday

call the white man, 'boss'
words ain't no loss
dollars and cents
moonshine for rents

paint it grey
getting drunk ain't making hay

nightmares and fever
hallucination swears,
the road to paradise
is too much of a price

paint it grey
this life is here to stay

wildfire

iano red
vas a little albino guy
vho just beat up the keys

e hit lots of bum notes
ut it didn't matter

iano red
ist stormed along
ie music was like it is

strikers - stay put

Sit down, you've got 'em beat.
Sit down, Sit down!
                    Maurice Sugar; song, 1937

one thing and one thing only
will beat *them* - sit down - sit in
don't move...

> strikers - stay put

they can't operate *their* machinery
when you are sat guarding it

> strikers - stay put

they have to get you out
of their building to stand a chance of beating you

> strikers - stay put

they will find *their* traditional methods of using
gangsters, machine guns, tear gas and violence
more difficult now you have solidarity

> strikers - stay put

one thing and one thing only
will beat *them* - sit down - sit in
don't move...

Brag

Mary Wells connected:
every dude received
the look and heard
the words: *My Guy.*

Songs can be personal:
was easy to think and boast;
Mary Wells sang,
My Guy to me.'

There was another brag
down at the Oxford Club
when you're high
on Mary Wells...

A pryle of Jacks -
cannot be beat:
car keys go in the pot-
winner takes all...

Emotion drained
the loser walks.
Mary Wells sings,
My Guy in her second show.

pleasure drome

a free for all
crossfire rhythm snarls
from stacked decks
of shaking speakers
as dry ice churns
smoke into pockets
of shimmering space
between limp dancers
whose spaced out
movements
serial kill time
in flickering
shadows of reality

Smoke Rings

The smoke rings
from Mr Ten Percent's
cigars were noticed.

He was the man - flash,
confident and respected;
he had the ear and the eye.

And the know how.
Mr Ten Percent was a spotter -
he took life

without hope from bars, gyms,
night-clubs and street corners
and gave it a chance;

made it a success - enough
times so it didn't matter
whether success

was big or small
it was worth ten percent
and enough of this slice

of the action took him
up and out of it - in cigar
smoke rings style.

Subway Conversation

a busker,
>   with a face pierced by shrapnel
>   courtesy of a winning skirmish
>   with the local benefit office,

loudly boasts,
>   to a sold out Big Issue seller
>   with an obligatory mongrel
>   and folded *queue here* sign,

of totally losing the plot
>   in a back street bar renowned
>   by the in-crowd as being
>   the best place to score.

The Party Party

If there is to be a revolution,
there must be a revolutionary party
Mao Tse -Tung - 1948

The party was held on
the flat roof of a council maisonette
in Wigan.

Around twenty
residents came, some for booze
some for company, some for the party.

Not that party,
the revolutionary party,
it was a political party, party,
a recruitment drive...

OK!

It didn't happen...
but dreams and realisation
of what it could have been,
still beat the crap out of today.

Ray

Too old to be a teenager
Ray had looks and style
to be part of the sixties.

His bedsit on the edge
of Longsight, Manchester
was a shrine to swinging.

Posters, concert programmes,
LP and book covers plus photographs
of the Great Beast decorated walls.

Ray's do it yourself four poster bed
had Indian silks trailing from the ceiling
to atmospherically curtain a love nest,

where sexual freedom
was enjoyed by amorous chicks
courtesy of Ray's seduction techniques.

Occasionally he trailed
gonorrhoea to VD clinics
for a touch of umbrella sadism.

Ray wanted to do it all
taste every aphrodisiac
of this psychedelic age.

He Beatled his hair,
played the top twenty,
rainbowed his clothes.

Saw all the bands, drank and danced
'til dawn before heading home in a Zephyr
with imitation tiger skin seat covers.

He puffed up and dabbled
with Benz and Dexes
had highs and lows

avelled on LSD
lew his cash
lew his mind.

uring his breakdown
ay met and married a psychologist,
venty years older than himself.

e still lives with her and her poodles
a semi-detached in Levenshulme.
ccasionally,

ay has a flashback
f heady days that don't seem
have anything to do with him.

Beat Women

*The truth of the matter is we don't understand our women;
we blame them and it's all our fault.*
                              Jack Kerouac

beat women
were feminist before the word
was pulverised by the sex
with a tag of bra burning

beat women
were an abstract of cool
who made it possible
to change savoir-faire forever

beat women
dare to create a life of creativity
leaving behind boredom and safety
of the typical American female

beat women
were their own persons
prominent artists, poets
intellectuals widening consciousness

Yes

his place
is moody lit
humid and out of it
everyone hangs loose

music here is rich
like corruption
it needs spreading
far and wide

a fusion of past,
present and future
the revolutionary
anthem of tomorrow

this is off the streets
straight in your face
off the back of welfare
customised reality

where urban virgins
hell bent on doing
what they do naturally
go over the edge of evolution

turn it up a notch
amplify gold into haze
prolong hot crazy nights
into dip-dap lazy days

Lay-By

Trees shield me from the road
darkness is my blanket
cupped hands behind my head
pillow dreams of getting away
escaping from the so called norm.

Solitude is very intense here,
silence stretches to invisible horizons.
I unscrew a bottle top
and take a long swig of wine,
shift position to aid circulation,

have a poetic thought
which I scribble in large letters
on a note pad kept for such moments.
It's too dark to read what I have written,
I wonder if I'll decipher it in the morning.

The stubble on my face
has leapt beyond seven o' clock shadow.
I think of Barbara who had the annoying habit
of rubbing my face stubble, just below the ear,
with her fingertips to made a rasping sound.

Toilets open early in the nearby town,
they have good wash-up facilities, although
I don't fancy a cold water shave first thing.

I swig wine until the bottle is empty,
wonder if I should dry brush my teeth
decide it does'nt matter if I do or I don't.
Besides I wouldn't want to frighten away
the warm hazy feel the wine has bequeathed.

I roll over unto my side
and turn my shirt collar up.
A barn owl hoots and I meditate
on the sound fading into peace.

wake up cramped and fur tongued,
urn on the car engine,
pen the car door, step outside,
tretch and piss.

old and relieved
get back into the car,
nd a fair size dog end in the ash tray
nd get some smoke into my lungs.

look
nto the car mirror
vith bloodshot eyes,
ase the gear stick into first
nd drive towards the road.

stop
o watch a fox slinking home
vith the blood
f a recent kill splashed
ver its chest.

Short Time

The amount she asked
for wasn't worth debating.
The words, *short time*
were a slur to his man hood...

This stale perfumed bitch;
had stuck her tongue
down his throat
and who after a grope
down the front of his jeans,
had declared,
he was a big boy,
in a voice to impress
his new drinking buddies.

He downed another beer
followed by a whisky chaser,
and was determined to show
her what he was made of:
he stumbled after her,
through the bar,
out of the fire exit
down the back alley
for a promised knee trembler.

The darkness,
and rush of cold night air
didn't affect him.
The knee slammed
between his legs, the cosh
to the back of the head
and the deft fingers
that lifted his bank roll
left him with a feeling,
even the hair of the dog
couldn't cure.

Street

On the corner of trash can alley:
where a junkie shot to fame,
they do the dance of the devil,
playing the chicken fives game.

Death casts a long shadow,
memories are fogged with pain,
acid trips are street corner news
and survival is a long term gain.

A chance from a mean south paw,
gives credit, another breath of hope,
remember that a shared dirty needle
cuts a sorry dozen finer than dope.

When the heat is closing in
two spots are a losing pair,
shivers back track the spine
and fingers clutch thin air.

Side walks are turf avenues,
borders of rival territory,
haunted by ghosts of war
former days of hell and glory.

Melting pots are poverty
seasoned with race and creed
tomorrow is another sentence
for prisoners of this breed.

Moving On

Thank God
the textile mill job was over.

Dust still floated in my lungs,
oil stains greased my jeans,

my pockets were as empty
as the day I started.

Time to move on.
Travel light,

get another job
in another location.

On the side of the main drag
I busted dawn with a cocky thumb.

Long distant lorry drivers
like company, they prefer females

but on a long trip
a catch hand can break monotony.

My lift was going to Manchester
one hitch, one ride to start one new life.

The journey was nicotine fuelled,
football was the opening conversation:

to support City or United was the question,
for and against

the blues and the reds
eased away lots of miles.

When the final whistle blew
his new topic was his sexual prowess.

was a one sided conversation
onducted as he drove with one hand.

is other hand indulged
self in a well practice rhythm.

silently prayed and made an apology
Sweet Mary, Mother of Jesus,

lutched my St Christopher and cultivated
sudden interest in the hard shoulder.

is loud climax of Oh God and Yes
as followed by well worn apologies:

n explanation of being an only child,
f being misunderstood by his wife,

f how diesel fumes affected the mind,
nd of too many long hours on the road.

said, I understood. The remainder
f the journey passed in silence.

Vhen we reached Manchester, he drove
ut of his way to take me into the city.

Ve parted company in Piccadilly: I thanked
im for the lift and he gave me his address,

nd an invitation
o look him up if I was ever in Rochdale.

beat reality

beat reality
is the dialect of sunsets
the breath of down and out days
the pronunciation of understanding

beat reality
is a nomadic existence
either on the road
or in the head

beat reality
is a journey of dreams
sailing over rocks into the wind
with rhythmic contraction and expansion

beat reality
is a counter culture crossing borders
uniting every colour and creed
in universal meditation

beat reality
is a chaos of thoughts
a confusion of creation
a hallucination of borrowed time

beat reality
is a stampede of clouds
the virgin silence of space
a science of new horizons

beat reality
is a taste of being
a wilderness symphony
an unscratchable wanderlust

beat reality
is a black and white
poetic rediscovery of self
on a shoe string jaunt

Inspired by Outlaws

eat reality
s a stream of utopia
lowing through arteries
o the pulse of peace

eat reality
s bare bone psyche
he purpose of meaning
he impact of sorrows and desires

eat reality
s sowing karma on barren ground
reward for immense consciousness
n unexpected vision

eat reality
s free love
nd giving love freely
o the only option is peace

eat reality
s a chrysalis
hat will go on to enjoy flights
f fancy with psychedelic wings

eat reality
s an echo of the ancients
he observation of today
nd the soul of tomorrow

Biography

Les Merton was born in 1944 in a remote cottage in Cornwall. His education comes mainly from the School of Hard Knocks and the University of Life.

In 2002, having achieved his ambition; to be a survivor many times over; he decided to step into the unknown and became the founder/editor of Poetry Cornwall/Bardhonyeth Kernow.

His poetry has been published widely in magazines, anthologies and on the internet and his A to Z of readings stretches from Altarnun to Zambia.

He has published three previous poetry collections:
Cornflakes and Toast
Light the Muse
As Yesterday Begins
and edited the anthology:
101 Poets for a Cornish Assembly

Les Merton was made a Bard of Gorseth Kernow in 2004 for services to Cornish Literature, his Bardic name is Map Hallow (Son of the Moors).

Beat Reality

by

Les Merton and The Moontones

is a 16 track CD that features **Inspired by Outlaws**
poems set to specially written music

Beat Reality can be ordered from
Palores Publications and Promotions
11a Penryn Street
Redruth
Cornwall
TR15 2SP

£10.00 plus £1 Postage & Package U.K.
£10.00 plus £2 Postage & Package R.O.W
Cheques in sterling made payable to:
Palores Publications
or
order by email from
les.merton@tesco.net
and pay by PayPal

The only thing that can save the world is the reclaiming of the awareness of the world. That's what poetry does.

Allen Ginsberg